Guillaume Apollinaire

OCEAN OF EARTH:
SELECTED POEMS

Translated from the French
by Matthew Geden

SurVision Books

First published in 2024 by
SurVision Books
Dublin, Ireland
www.survisionmagazine.com

Translations © Matthew Geden, 2024

Cover image and design © SurVision Books, 2024

ISBN: 978-1-912963-54-6

This book is in copyright. No part of this publication may be reproduced, stored in a retrieval system or transmitted in any form or by any means without the prior permission in writing from the publisher.

Acknowledgements

Some of the poems included in this collection, or their versions, originally appeared in *Autumn: Twenty Poems by Guillaume Apollinaire* transl. by Matthew Geden. Lapwing Publications, Belfast, 2003.

CONTENTS

Ocean of Earth	5
Twilight	6
The Cavalier's Farewell	8
Annie	9
Clotilde	10
White Snow	11
The Farewell	12
The Door	13
The Gypsy	14
The Night Wind	15
Autumn	16
Rose	17
Sign	18
The Lady	19
Moonlight	20
An Evening	21
1909	22
At the Santé	24
Sick Autumn	28
The Carp	30
The Cat	31
Hotels	32
Hunting Horns	34
From *Song of the Unloved*	35
The Recaptured Curl	37
War	38
Always	39
Wedding	40
Hotel	41

Ocean of Earth

For G. de Chirico

I've built a house in the middle of the ocean
Its windows are rivers coursing from my eyes
Octopuses overrun the walls
You can hear their triple heartbeat and their beaks
   banging on the windows
           Damp house
           Burning house
           Quick season
           Singing season
      Warplanes are laying eggs
      Watch out we're dropping anchor
Watch out for the spilled ink
It's good that you came down from the sky
The honeysuckle sky clambers up
The terrestrial octopuses pulsate
And so many of us are digging our own graves
Pale octopuses of chalky waves o octopuses with pale beaks
Around the house is the ocean you know so well
And it never rests

Twilight

For Mademoiselle Marie Laurencin

Grazed by shadows of the dead
Where the day dies on the grass
The harlequin undresses
Admires her body in the pool

A charlatan in the twilight
Boasts of the tricks to be done
The sky is colourless and set
With constellations pale like milk

From the platform the harlequin
Greets the audience
Magicians from Bohemia
Some fairies and sorcerers

He unhooks a star
Offers it with outstretched arms
Whilst a hanged man's feet
Beat time on the cymbals

The blind man rocks a pretty child
The doe passes with her fawns
The sad-eyed dwarf looks on
At the magical growth of the harlequin

The Cavalier's Farewell

My God! what a wonderful war
With its songs its hours of leisure
I have polished this ring
The wind joins in your sighs

Goodbye! the bugle is calling
He vanished around the corner
And died there while she
Laughed at the unexpectedness of fate

Annie

On the coast of Texas
Between Mobile and Galveston
There's a big garden full of roses
It also contains a house
Which is one big rose

A woman often walks there
All alone in the garden
And when I pass between the lime trees
We stare at each other

This woman is a Mennonite
Neither her roses nor her clothes have buttons
Two are missing from my jacket
The woman and I almost follow the same religion

Clotilde

The anemone and the columbine
Have pushed up in the garden
Where melancholy lies
Between love and disdain

There were also our shadows
Absorbed into the night
Darkened by the sun
Before they disappeared

The gods of living water
Let loose their hair
And you will have to follow
This beautiful shadow you long for

White Snow

Angels angels in the sky
One is an officer
One is a cook
The others sing

Handsome officer the colour of sky
Soft spring long after Christmas
Decorate yourself with the beautiful sun
        The beautiful sun

The cook plucks geese
        Ah! snow falls
        Falls and I don't have
My beloved in my arms

The Farewell

I gathered this spray of heather
Don't forget autumn is dead
We won't pass this way again
Scent of time spray of heather
Never forget I'm waiting for you

The Door

The hotel door smiles terribly
What does it mean to me mother
To work as though nothing exists
Pi-mus coupled swim in deep sad water
Yesterday fresh angels disembarked in Marseilles
I hear a distant song die and fade away
I am humble and worth nothing

Child I've given you all that I've cultivated

The Gypsy

The gypsy forewarned
Both our lives frustrated by the nights
We bade her farewell and then then
Hope emerged from holes in the ground

Love heavy as a circus bear
Danced on its hind legs at our command
And the bluebird lost its feathers
And friars lost their prayers

One knows very well one is damned
But the hope of love along the way
Makes us think of going hand in hand
To what the gypsy had foretold

The Night Wind

Oh! The pine tops creak as they collide
And you can also hear the wind moan
And triumphant voices from the nearby river
Elves laughing at the wind or into the gusts
Attis Attis Attis charming and dishevelled
It's you that the elves scoff at in the night
Because your pines crash down in the gothic wind
The forest trembles like an ancient army
Whose spears in the pines shake and bend
The deserted villages meditate now
Like virgins the elderly and poets
And don't respond to anyone
Not even when their pigeons are pounced on by vultures

Autumn

In the mist a broken peasant and his ox
Pass slowly in the autumn fog
Shrouding the shamefully poor hamlets

And the peasant goes away singing
A song of love and infidelity
That tells of a ring and a broken heart

Oh! Autumn the autumn kills the summer
In the mist two grey shadows pass

Rose

For André Derain

Standing for ages on the steps
Of the house where a woman entered
She who I'd followed for two
Good hours in Amsterdam
My fingers threw away kisses

But the canal was deserted
So too the quay and no-one saw
How my kisses found their way
To her whom I have given my life
A day lasting more than two hours

I named her Rose
Allowing me remember
Her mouth as a Dutch flower
Then slowly I left
To search for the Rose of the World

Sign

I submit to the powers of Autumn
So I love fruit I hate flowers
I rue each of the kisses I give
Like a walnut tree confides its grief to the wind

My constant Autumn my inner season
The hands of last year's lovers strewn on your soil
A wife follows me my deadly shadow
The doves this evening take their last flight

The Lady

Knock Knock He closed his door
The garden lilies are withered
What is this death that's swept along

You came to tap at his door
      And scurry scurry
      Scurry small mouse

Moonlight

The moon like honey over the lips of madmen
The orchards and towns tonight are greedy
The stars are imitated by bees
The honey light drips from trellises
And suddenly sweetness falls from the sky
Each moonbeam a ray of honey
And full of adventure I hide
Afraid of the fiery sting of the star
Which poured disappointing light into my hands
And stole the honeylight from the rose of the winds

An Evening

An eagle descended from the archangels white sky
        And you sustain me
How long will you let these lights tremble
        Pray pray for me

The town is metallic and is the only star
        Sunk in your blue eyes
When the trams trundled they spurted pale fires
        Onto mangy birds

And all that trembled in your eyes was dreamed
        And one man drank
Under gaslight red like fungus
        Your sleeves coiled up

The actor sticks out his tongue at his audience
        A ghost has killed himself
The apostle hangs from the fig tree and slowly drools
        We gamble on love

The bells clearly announced your birth
        Look
The lanes are blooming and the palms advancing
        Towards you

1909

The lady wore a dress
Of violet silk
And her golden tunic
Was made up of two sections
Fastened at the shoulder

Her eyes danced like angels
She laughed she laughed
Her face was the colours of France
Blue eyes white teeth and lips so red
Her face was the colours of France

She wore a low-cut dress
And hair styled like Récamier's
With beautiful bare arms

Shall we never hear the stroke of midnight

The lady dressed in violet silk
And the golden tunic
With the low-cut dress
Showed off her curls

Her golden hairband
And trailed her small buckled shoes

She was so beautiful
You wouldn't have dared love her

I loved the foul women in the enormous districts
Where new ones were born every day
Iron was their blood the flame their brain
I loved I loved the workers and their machines
Wealth and beauty are only dross
That woman was so beautiful
She frightened me

At the Santé

I

Before entering my cell
I had to strip naked
And a sinister voice sang
Guillaume what have you become

I am Lazarus entering the tomb
At the exit as he did
Farewell farewell the songs rang round
Farewell to the years and the young girls

II

No I am no longer
      Myself
I am number fifteen
      In the eleventh

Sunlight filters through
      The window panes
Its light on my lines
      Clowns

    It dances on the paper
        I hear
    Someone's footsteps strike
        Above me

III

In a pit like a bear
Each morning I pace
Around around always around
The sky is blue as a chain
In a pit like a bear
Each morning I pace

In the cell beside mine
The tap is dripping
With his keys jangling
The jailer comes and goes
In the cell beside mine
The tap is dripping

IV

How bored I am between these walls
        Whitewashed
A fly on the paper with tiny steps
        Wanders through my words

What will become of me Lord who knows my pain
        You gave it me
Take pity on my dry eyes my pallor
        The scrape of my chained chair

And all the poor hearts beating in prison
        Love my companion
Particularly pity my failing reason
        As despair takes over

V

The hours pass
As slowly as a funeral

You will weep for the hour
Which passed too quickly
As all hours do

VI

I hear the city sounds
A prisoner with no horizon
I see nothing but a hostile sky
And my prison walls

The day ends here lighting
A lamp in the prison
We are alone in my cell
Beautiful light Dear reason

September 1911

Sick Autumn

Sick autumn and adored
You die when storms attack the roses
When snow falls
In the orchards

Poor autumn
Die in whiteness and in wealth
Of snow and ripe fruit
In the depths of the sky
Hawks hover
Over green-haired river nymphs and dwarves
Who never loved

At the distant edges
The stags have bayed

And when I love o season when I love your rumours
Fruit falling without being gathered
The wind and the fores sobbing
All their tears in autumn leaf by leaf

Leaves
Trampled
A train
On the rails
Life
Passes by

The Carp

In your fish-tanks, in your ponds,
Carp, how long you survive!
Has death forgotten you,
Melancholy fish?

The Cat

In my house I wish for:
A reasonable woman,
A cat busy among books,
Some friends for every season
Without whom I cannot live.

Hotels

Each room is widowed
Every one is alone
People pass through
Stay a while

The manager suspects
He won't be paid
I turn around
Like a spinning top

The sound of cabs
My ugly neighbour
Smokes an acrid
English tobacco

Oh La Vallière
She limps and laughs
At my prayers
My bedside table

And all together
In this hotel
We know the languages
Of Babel

We double-lock
Our doors
Each one alone
The one true love

Hunting Horns

Our story is noble and tragic
Like a tyrant's mask
No random drama or magic
No indifferent detail
Could render our love pathetic

Thomas de Quincy drinks
The sweet chaste poisoned opium
Goes to his poor Anne dreaming
Move on move on since all passes
I will return often

Memories are hunting horns
Their song dies in the wind

From *Song of the Unloved*

For Paul Léautaud

    And I sang this song
    In 1903 not knowing
    That my love resembled
    The beautiful Phoenix dead
    In the evening reborn by morning

    One night in the London fog
    A young punk reminiscent
    Of my love appeared before me
    When he looked at me
    I glanced down in shame

    I followed that troublemaker
    As he whistled hands in pockets
    The Red Sea parted
    Between the houses
    I the Pharaoh and he the Jews

Let these waves of bricks fall
If you were unloved
If you are not my true love
I am the King of Egypt
His incestuous wife and his army

At the turn of the burning street
All its fiery facades
Bled into wounds of fog
And even the shop fronts lamented
A woman who looked like him

She had the same vacant look
And scar on her naked neck
As she fell out of the pub
And in her fall I knew
The fakery of love itself

The Recaptured Curl

He rediscovers in his memory
The curl of chestnut hair
Does it remind you not to trust
In our two strange destinies

From the Boulevard da la Chapelle
From pretty Montmartre and Auteuil
I remember she murmured
The day I passed through your door

Then falling like autumn
The curl of my memory
And our destiny which stuns you
Bound to the dying of the day

War

The central combat zone
      Contact by listening
Or fire in the direction of "noises heard"
      The young men of the class of 1915
And these electric fences
So don't cry about the horror of war
Before it we only had the surface
Of earth and sea
After it we will have the abyss
The underground and the free space above
Men of the tiller
Afterwards Afterwards
We will take all the joys
Of the victors who rest
      Women Games Factories Commerce
      Industry Agriculture Metal
      Fire Crystal Speed
Voice Look Touch apart
And together from the far-away touch
Even further away
From beyond the earth

Always

For Madame Faure-Favier

                Always
We go further without ever advancing
And from planet to planet
From nebula to nebula
Don Juan of a thousand and three comets
Without even leaving the earth
Seek new strengths
And take ghosts seriously

And so many universes are forgotten
Who are the great forgetters
Who can make us forget this or that part of the world
Where is Christopher Columbus to whom we owe
      the forgetting of a continent
                To lose
But to truly lose
To leave room for discovery
                        To lose
Life to find Victory

Wedding

For one who is on the seashore

Love married absence one summer night;
So that my love for your youth
Slowly accompanies its wife, your absence,
Who, gentle and calm, shows the way in silence.
And the love which arrived at ocean shores,
Where nudes make the sky seem Greek,
Weeps to be a god again and yet unknown,
This jealous god as only gods may be.

Hotel

My room is shaped like a cage
The sun slips its arm through the window
But I want to smoke make mirages
Sunlight lights my cigarette
I don't want to work I want to smoke

Selected Poetry Titles Published by SurVision Books

Contemporary Tangential Surrealist Poetry: An Anthology
Edited by Tony Kitt
ISBN 978-1-912963-44-7

Invasion: An Anthology of Ukrainian Poetry about the War
Edited by Tony Kitt
ISBN 978-1-912963-32-4

Matthew Geden. *Fruit*
(New Poetics: Ireland)
ISBN 978-1-912963-16-4

John W. Sexton. *Inverted Night*
(New Poetics: Ireland)
ISBN 978-1-912963-05-8

Afric McGlinchey. *The Throat-Bird*
(New Poetics: Ireland)
ISBN 978-1-912963-53-9

Tony Kitt. *The Magic Phlute*
(New Poetics: Ireland)
ISBN 978-1-912963-08-9

Noel King. *Suitable Music for a View*
(New Poetics: Ireland)
ISBN 978-1-912963-46-1

Ciaran O'Driscoll. *Angel Hour*
ISBN 978-1-912963-27-0

Order our books from http://survisionmagazine.com

www.ingramcontent.com/pod-product-compliance
Lightning Source LLC
Chambersburg PA
CBHW061308040426
42444CB00010B/2559